NEWSMAKERS

# TAYLOR SWIFT

## MUSIC INDUSTRY LEADER

BY ALICIA Z. KLEPEIS

Core Library

An Imprint of Abdo Publishing
abdobooks.com

Cover image: Taylor Swift attended the Toronto International Film Festival for the screening of *All Too Well: The Short Film*.

abdobooks.com



Printed in the United States of America, North Mankato, Minnesota.
102024
012025

THIS BOOK CONTAINS RECYCLED MATERIALS

Cover Photo: Amy Sussman/Getty Images Entertainment/Getty Images
Interior Photo: Gilbert Flores/Billboard/Getty Images, 4–5; John Mabangalo/Getty Images Sport/Getty Images, 8; Kevin Mazur/WireImage/Getty Images, 10–11, 18–19; Dee Browning/Shutterstock Images, 13; Jason Kempin/Getty Images Entertainment/Getty Images, 16; Red Line Editorial, 20; Don Arnold/WireImage/Getty Images, 22, 43; Kevin Mazur/TAS18/Getty Images Entertainment/Getty Images, 26–27; Erika Goldring/FilmMagic/Getty Images, 31; Kevin Mazur/Getty Images for The Recording Academy/Getty Images Entertainment/Getty Images, 32, 34–35, 45; Christopher Polk/Penske Media/Getty Images, 37 (left); Fernando Leon/TAS23/Getty Images for TAS Rights Management/Getty Images Entertainment/Getty Images, 37 (center); Aldara Zarraoa/Getty Images for TAS Rights Management/Getty Images Entertainment/Getty Images, 37 (right); Shutterstock Images, 40 (record, tickets, microphone, guitar, movie clapper), 40 (Grammy)

Editor: Katharine Hale
Series Designer: Marley Richmond

**Library of Congress Control Number: 2024938388**

**Publisher's Cataloging-in-Publication Data**

Names: Klepeis, Alicia Z., author.
Title: Taylor Swift: music industry leader / by Alicia Z. Klepeis
Other title: music industry leader
Description: Minneapolis, Minnesota: ABDO Publishing, 2025 | Series: Newsmakers | Includes online resources and index.
Identifiers: ISBN 9781098295738 (lib. bdg.) | ISBN 9798384916734 (ebook)
Subjects: LCSH: Swift, Taylor, 1989---Juvenile literature. | Singers--Biography--Juvenile literature. | Women musicians--Biography--Juvenile literature. | Songwriters--Biography--Juvenile literature. | Popular music --Juvenile literature. | Businesswomen--Biography--Juvenile literature.
Classification: DDC 781.642--dc23

# CONTENTS

CHAPTER ONE

# BREAKING RECORDS

All eyes were on Taylor Swift as she strolled down the red carpet during the Grammy Awards on February 4, 2024. Her shimmery gown and long gloves dazzled celebrities and reporters. A clock on her choker necklace was set to 12:00. This was a nod to her *Midnights* album, which had been nominated for two awards.

All evening, Swift cheered on her fellow artists. But in many ways, the night belonged to her. *Midnights* won the Grammy for Best

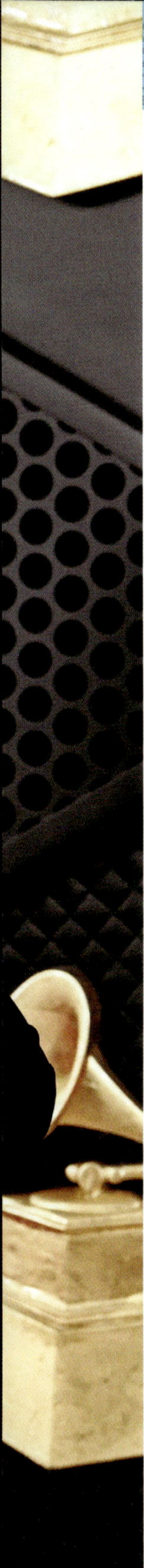

**Taylor Swift's Best Pop Vocal Album Grammy for *Midnights* was her thirteenth Grammy win.**

Pop Vocal Album. During her acceptance speech, Swift shared big news. Her newest album, *The Tortured Poets Department*, would be released on April 19.

But the night wasn't over yet. One of the biggest honors of the Grammys is Album of the Year. Swift had won this award for her albums *Fearless*, *1989*, and *Folklore*. Legendary singer Celine Dion came onstage to announce this year's winner. It was *Midnights*! Despite all her previous awards, Swift looked truly shocked. She was the first person ever to win this award four times.

### "CHRISTMAS TREE FARM"

**In December 2019, Swift released a song called "Christmas Tree Farm." The music video features footage from her childhood. One clip shows a tiny Taylor looking through her Christmas stocking. Another shows her opening a guitar.**

## A CREATIVE CHILDHOOD

Taylor Alison Swift was born in Reading, Pennsylvania, on December 13, 1989. She grew up on a Christmas tree farm in nearby Wyomissing.

She lived with her parents, Andrea and Scott. Her younger brother, Austin, was born in 1992.

Taylor loved music and being onstage. She was a huge fan of country artist LeAnn Rimes. She also admired Shania Twain and the Chicks, then called the Dixie Chicks.

Taylor's parents supported her musical ambitions. They drove her to perform at cafés and karaoke contests. At ten years old, Taylor saw a TV show about country star Faith Hill. The show said Hill moved to Nashville, Tennessee, when she was 19. Nashville was the center of the country music industry. Taylor wanted to be a part of it. She begged her parents to take her there.

## USING MUSIC TO ESCAPE

When she was 12, Taylor wrote a song called "The Outside." It was about being lonely and not fitting in at school. Her own pain served as inspiration in the songwriting process. Creating music helped her escape from a tough time in middle school.

**Before getting a record deal, Taylor sang the National Anthem at as many events as possible to get in front of a crowd. She continued singing for Pennsylvania sports teams in her early career.**

When Taylor was 11, she visited Nashville. She had recorded demo tapes, which are recordings designed to show a musician's work. Her mom waited in the car while Taylor left the tapes at major record labels. This trip didn't result in a record deal, but the rejection motivated her to keep trying.

At 12, Taylor learned to play the guitar. She would play until her fingers bled. Her mom taped them up for her. Taylor's star was rising. She sang the national anthem at a Philadelphia 76ers National Basketball Association (NBA) game in 2002. More than 20,000 basketball fans were looking on. But even bigger things were on the horizon.

# STRAIGHT TO THE SOURCE

On February 4, 2024, Swift won a Grammy Award for Album of the Year. During her acceptance speech, she spoke to the audience:

> *I would love to tell you that this is the best moment of my life, but I feel this happy when I finish a song, or when I crack the code to a bridge I love, or when I'm shotlisting a music video, or when I'm rehearsing with my dancers or my band, or getting ready to go to Tokyo to play a show. For me the award is the work. All I wanna do is keep being able to do this. I love it so much, it makes me so happy.*

Source: Douglas Markowitz. "2024 Grammys: Taylor Swift Makes Grammy History with Fourth Album of the Year Win for 'Midnights.'" *Grammy Awards*, 4 Feb. 2024, grammy.com. Accessed 18 Mar. 2024.

## WHAT'S THE BIG IDEA?

**Read this section of Swift's speech carefully. What is the main idea she is expressing? Which details support this idea? Name two or three details Swift uses to support her main idea.**

CHAPTER TWO

# COUNTRY MUSIC CHARMER

Taylor worked hard to achieve her goals. She wrote her own songs, returned to Nashville, and kept trying to break into the industry. When she was 13, RCA Records offered her a development deal. This is when a record company agrees to watch musical artists but doesn't promise them an album. Instead, the artists turn in songs for consideration. After a year, the record company decides if it wants to keep watching the artists, drop them, or make an album.

**Taylor and her mom attended the 2007 CMT Music Awards in Nashville. Nashville is known as Music City.**

Getting a development deal was huge. Taylor got to share her songs with industry professionals. But after a year, she left. RCA wasn't willing to give Taylor a record deal yet. She also wasn't sure RCA would support her goal of singing only songs she had written. Her songwriting confidence was well-founded. When she was 14, SONY/ATV Publishing offered Taylor a songwriting contract. Staff songwriters get help selling their songs in exchange for publishing rights. Taylor was the youngest songwriter they'd ever signed.

Taylor's family moved to Nashville in 2003. Songwriting was always her top priority. She said that if she didn't write songs, she wouldn't sing. When Taylor was in eighth grade, her mom would pick her up after school and bring her to work with other songwriters in downtown Nashville. There, Taylor would share her thoughts on everything from boys to school. Then she'd go home to do her homework.

Taylor's skills as a songwriter were gaining attention. But she still hadn't landed a record deal.

Country stars such as Faith Hill and Garth Brooks were also discovered at the Bluebird Cafe.

Everything changed in late 2004 when Taylor sang several of her songs at the Bluebird Cafe. After the show, record executive Scott Borchetta approached her. He wanted her to join his record label. In 2005, Taylor signed on with Borchetta's new label, Big Machine Records. The following year, Taylor's first album was released. *Taylor Swift* was a country album. Taylor worked on its first single, "Tim McGraw," with songwriter Liz Rose in her after-school sessions. It made the Top 10 on the *Billboard* Hot Country Songs chart.

Because Big Machine Records was a new label, Taylor had to be creative about spreading her message.

## LIZ ROSE

**As a teenager, Taylor collaborated with songwriter Liz Rose. Rose admired Taylor's brilliance, focus, and fun spirit. She edited the lyrics for the hit song "Tim McGraw," which became Taylor's first single and went platinum. Rose and Taylor worked on a total of 16 songs together.**

One way she did this was through MySpace, an early social media platform. It helped Taylor spread the word about who she was as a person and an artist.

Touring was another way Taylor promoted her music. She was the opening act for other country musicians. She even opened for some dates on Tim McGraw and Faith Hill's Soul2Soul II Tour. Tours brought Taylor's music to a bigger audience.

To accommodate her busy travel schedule, Taylor started homeschooling while in high school. In her senior year, she won the Horizon Award at the Country Music Association Awards (CMAs) in November 2007. This award is given to an artist who voters believe has shown the most career growth in the previous year.

She released her second album, *Fearless*, in November 2008. It was another country album.

## AWARD SHOWS

The year 2009 brought many firsts for Swift. In February, she performed at the Grammys for the first time. And in April, Swift launched her first headlining tour. It started with a sold-out show in Evansville, Indiana. Taylor was now a true superstar.

### UPS AND DOWNS

One day, 17-year-old Taylor came home to find her mom sobbing. Taylor had been booked to open for superstar Kenny Chesney on his summer tour. But because a beer company sponsored the tour, she was too young to participate. Her mom was upset about this missed opportunity. But when Taylor turned 18 a few months later, Chesney sent her a card. He apologized about the tour and included a big check. Taylor gave her band bonuses, paid for tour buses, and continued working toward her dreams.

Not every awards ceremony went smoothly. In September 2009, Swift

Swift said that being fearless isn't the same as being unafraid. Instead, it's being scared but still living life fully and taking risks.

was at the MTV Video Music Awards (VMAs). She had just won Best Video by a Female Artist for "You Belong with Me." Singer Kanye West rushed the stage and interrupted her acceptance speech, saying Beyoncé should have won instead. Swift was stunned into silence. Though the experience was hurtful, she pushed through to perform the song live later in the evening. When Beyoncé won the award for Video of the Year, she invited Swift onstage to finish her acceptance speech.

It wasn't long before Swift had a more joyful award experience. In January 2010, she won her first Grammy for the country song "White Horse." She won three more Grammys that night, including Album of the Year for *Fearless*. *Fearless* had already won Album of the Year at the CMAs and the Academy of Country Music Awards. But the all-genre Grammy win proved Swift's appeal reached beyond country music.

## FIGHTING BACK

Many critics thought Swift didn't actually write her songs. She was determined to prove them wrong. When she released *Speak Now* in October 2010, it had no cowriters. The album went platinum in its first week.

*Red* released in October 2012. Swift said the color red represents intense emotions such as passion and anger. Swift varied the feeling of each song on the album, from loud and chaotic to gentle guitar strumming. *Red* signaled a transition in Swift's music. Some songs were country. But others crossed over to pop. "We Are Never Ever Getting Back Together," released ahead of the album in August, became Swift's first No. 1 on the *Billboard* Hot 100 chart.

WE'LL PAY
FEES

CHAPTER THREE

# BECOMING A POP ICON

Throughout her twenties, Swift continued to try new things. In the spring of 2014, Swift moved from Nashville to New York City. As she worked on her new album, Swift felt strongly about changing musical directions. Her favorite song from *Red* was the pop anthem "I Knew You Were Trouble." She wanted to build on that success and create something different from anything she had done before. The new *1989* became Swift's first official pop album.

**Swift performed a *1989* concert in New York City's Times Square. Swift said she enjoyed focusing on one genre for the album.**

## THE *1989* SECRET SESSIONS

The *1989* Secret Sessions were a way Swift rewarded her most loyal fans. This map shows the locations of these special events. Sessions were at Swift's homes, her mom's house in Nashville, and a London hotel. What do you notice about the locations?

But before the whole world heard *1989*, Swift scoured the internet to find her most loyal fans. She invited them to secret *1989* listening parties. Swift baked cookies for her fans and sat with them in her living room. She played the entire album for them and explained the stories behind the tracks.

The lead single from *1989* was "Shake It Off." It came out in August 2014, debuting at No. 1 on the

*Billboard* Hot 100.

The full *1989* album was released on October 27. It sold more than 1.2 million copies in its first week.

## SHAKING IT OFF

Swift has talked about fighting sexism throughout her career. People often comment on her dating life. They say Swift writes songs only about ex-boyfriends. Swift pointed out that male artists do this without criticism. She thinks men in power are intimidated by her success. Swift told fans that she can't control what people say about her, but she can control how she reacts. This inspired her song "Shake It Off."

## TAKING ON STREAMING

Swift is both a brilliant musician and a savvy businesswoman. She was unhappy with how the music streaming platform Spotify paid artists. Spotify allows users to listen to music for free in exchange for listening to advertisements. Users can buy a subscription to remove ads. On average, artists received under one cent per stream. In November 2014, Swift removed all her music from Spotify.

**Swift later collaborated with Apple Music on a documentary. Called *The 1989 World Tour Live*, the film released exclusively on the streaming service in 2015.**

Swift also challenged Apple Music. At its launch in June 2015, Apple offered new subscribers a three-month free trial. During this time, Apple didn't pay artists for their music. Swift wrote that artists should be paid during this trial period. In protest, she said Apple would not be able to stream *1989*. Within a day, Apple agreed to pay artists during the free trial.

In 2017, Swift was getting ready to release a new album. In addition, *1989* had sold ten million copies. To celebrate this milestone, Swift made her music available on all streaming services, including Spotify.

## SHARING FEELINGS

Swift's new album came in the wake of a scandal. Swift and Kanye West had made up after the 2009 VMAs. But in 2016, West released a song with rude lyrics about Swift. She publicly criticized him for it. But West's wife, Kim Kardashian West, revealed another side of the story. She shared clips of a phone call in which Swift approved the lyrics. Swift said she hadn't heard all the lyrics, but many people felt she was not being fully honest about the situation. Swift faced backlash, and she ended up taking some time away from the public eye in the aftermath.

## TAKING A STAND

In 2013, Swift took a photo with radio DJ David Mueller. During the photo, she said he grabbed her underneath her skirt. Swift's team reported Mueller to the station where he worked. Mueller was fired. He sued Swift, saying the accusation was false and had ruined his career. Swift countersued Mueller for sexual assault. She testified in court in August 2017 and won the case. Mueller was ordered to pay one dollar. Swift chose the amount to show that the case was not about money but about standing up for herself and other victims.

In August 2017, Swift released the first single from her sixth album, *Reputation*. Titled "Look What You Made Me Do," the song was dark and sassy, different from her previous work. The full album dropped that November. Swift said making the album helped her sort out her feelings during a difficult time.

# STRAIGHT TO THE SOURCE

In 2014, Swift wrote a piece for the *Wall Street Journal*. In it, she shared her hopes for the future of the music industry:

> *My hope for the future, not just in the music industry, but in every young girl I meet . . . is that they all realize their worth and ask for it.*
>
> *Music is art, and art is important and rare. Important, rare things are valuable. Valuable things should be paid for. It's my opinion that music should not be free, and my prediction is that individual artists and their labels will someday decide what an album's price point is. I hope they don't underestimate themselves or undervalue their art.*

Source: Taylor Swift. "For Taylor Swift, the Future of Music Is a Love Story." *Wall Street Journal*, 7 July 2014, wsj.com. Accessed 2 May 2024.

## CONSIDER YOUR AUDIENCE

After reviewing this passage closely, adapt it for a different audience, such as younger friends or your parents. Write a blog post conveying this same information for the new audience. How is your post different from the original text, and why?

rep
FEARLESS
CERTIFIED
DIAMOND

CHAPTER FOUR

# TAKING CHARGE

In 2018, Swift's contract at Big Machine Records was set to expire. She began talking with other record companies. She was looking for more creative and financial freedom than she had before. In November 2018, she joined Republic Records, part of Universal Music Group. A major factor in Swift's decision was ownership of her new master recordings. This was something she didn't have for her previous albums. Master recordings are the original recordings of songs.

**Big Machine Records president Scott Borchetta, *right*, presented Swift with plaques celebrating her album sales in July 2018.**

Whoever owns a song's master controls its licensing, or how it can be used in TV, movies, and more. Typically a recording label owns an artist's masters. But some artists agree to different contracts to own them.

## *MISS AMERICANA*

**Released in January 2020, *Miss Americana* is a documentary about Taylor Swift's life. It focuses on the period after she won three Grammy Awards for *1989*. In one scene, she finds out that *Reputation* wasn't nominated for any Grammys. Other topics covered include learning to share her political opinions, her fight with Kanye West, and her struggles with an eating disorder.**

## POLITICAL AND POSITIVE

Human rights were another focus of Swift's attention. At the start of her career, she did not share her political opinions. But by 2018, she became more vocal on politics. Swift saw it as her responsibility to support candidates who fought for human rights. She shared her beliefs openly in person and on social media, speaking out against systemic racism and discrimination based on gender or sexual orientation.

Swift also supported marginalized communities through her music and performances. The video for "ME!" came out in April 2019. The first single on her album *Lover*, the song was a celebration of individuality. It featured many rainbows, a nod to her being an ally to the LGBTQ community. The full *Lover* album was released that August. Its upbeat vibe celebrated love. The song "You Need to Calm Down" supported the LGBTQ community through its lyrics and video.

All summer long, Swift encouraged her fans to support the Equality Act. This bill

## THE EQUALITY ACT

**Swift has been working for years to support the Equality Act. The bill would apply to many areas of life, including housing, employment, education, federal funding, and the jury system. The Equality Act passed the House of Representatives in February 2021, but by 2024 it still hadn't passed in the Senate.**

would prohibit discrimination based on sex, sexual orientation, and gender identity. Swift launched a petition asking the US Senate to pass the bill. In just days, more than 500,000 people had signed it.

## RE-RECORDING ALBUMS

Swift had clashed with music industry manager Scooter Braun in the past, calling him a bully. In June 2019, Braun's company, Ithaca Holdings, bought Big Machine Records. This purchase included the rights to Swift's first six albums. That meant anytime someone paid for one of these songs, Braun would profit.

Swift decided to re-record her earlier albums. This would let her regain full control over her music. It would also allow her to update songs and release songs that were not originally on the albums. Braun would still profit off the old masters. But Swift hoped to push them out of use with the new recordings.

**Swift has won 65 BMI Awards, which recognize songwriting. As a songwriter, Swift still has some control over her master recordings. She has to give approval for them to be licensed.**

BMI
BMI
BMI
Robert J. Burton
Liz Rose
You Belong With Me
Most Performed Country
2010

*Folklore* won the Grammy Award for Album of the Year in 2021.

## PANDEMIC PRODUCTIVITY

Swift was supposed to go on tour in 2020. But like the rest of the world, she saw her plans derailed by the COVID-19 pandemic. Many concerts were canceled, including Swift's. However, Swift turned this tough phase into a creative period. She released *Folklore* in July 2020. Its folk music influences leaned much more toward indie music than her recent pop albums. In December 2020, Swift released *Evermore*, which she saw as a sister or companion album to *Folklore*.

Swift's pandemic productivity continued into 2021. She released *Fearless (Taylor's Version)* in April. It became the first re-recorded album ever to top the *Billboard* charts. Her second re-release, *Red (Taylor's Version)*, debuted at No. 1 on the *Billboard* 200 chart that November. Its original version in 2008 had done the same.

## FURTHER EVIDENCE

**Chapter Four talks about Taylor Swift gaining control of her full catalog of music. What was a main point in this chapter? What evidence supports this point? Watch the video at the website below. Does the information on the website support the main point of the chapter? Does it present new evidence?**

### HOW DOLLY PARTON RECLAIMED HER CAREER

**abdocorelibrary.com/taylor-swift**

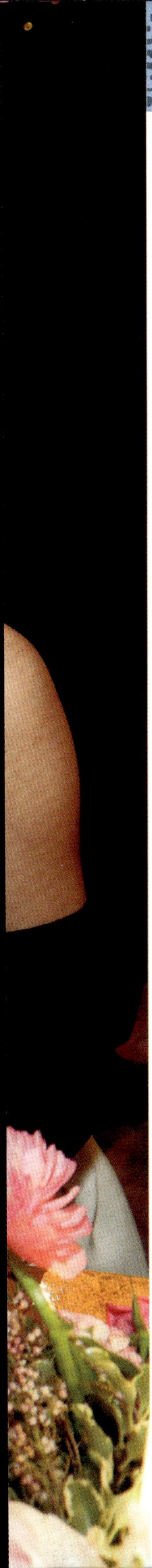

CHAPTER FIVE

# ON TOP OF THE WORLD

Swift continued to create new albums and re-record old ones. In October 2022, she released her tenth studio album, *Midnights*. Its 13 tracks include several collaborations, including "Snow on the Beach" with Lana Del Rey. Swift considers 13 to be her lucky number.

Swift fans, often called Swifties, were thrilled with all the music Swift was releasing. But they wanted a chance to see her live. It had been four years since her *Reputation* tour.

**Swift and Lana Del Rey, *left*, attended the 2024 Grammy Awards ceremony together.**

Swift announced her Eras Tour in November 2022. She would play in 20 cities across the United States. Swift later announced an international tour with additional shows in the United States. She planned to play 152 shows in 54 cities around the world. Fans flocked to the internet to buy tickets. So many people were online that the Ticketmaster website crashed. More than two million tickets sold in the first day.

Swift kicked off the Eras Tour in Glendale, Arizona, on March 17, 2023. She played 53 shows, ending in Los Angeles, California, on August 9. Swift launched the

## ECONOMY BOOSTER

**The Eras Tour had economic benefits for host cities. On average, a tour-going Swiftie contributes about $1,300 to a local economy. This money is spent on transportation, hotels, restaurants, merchandise, and even beauty services. In addition, Swift donated to food banks in cities along the tour. While extra police patrols and security are added costs for the host city, they are minimal compared with the benefits.**

**During the Eras Tour, Swift appeared in a sparkly bodysuit to celebrate her *Lover* era. For *Reputation*, Swift dazzled in a black-and-red outfit. Swift played a moss-covered piano for her *Evermore* era, creating a woodsy vibe.**

international tour on August 24 with a show in Mexico City, Mexico. She visited South America, Asia, Australia, and Europe.

Each concert lasted more than three hours. The shows paid tribute to each musical era of her career. Swift performed more than 40 songs at every show.

She also played different surprise songs. Sometimes celebrity guests joined her onstage. Elaborate costumes and set designs were part of the Eras Tour magic.

## MOVIEMAKER, RECORD BREAKER

Swift knew that many fans who wanted to see the Eras Tour had never gotten the chance. She released a concert movie to help those fans feel as if they were there. *Taylor Swift: The Eras Tour* was filmed during three shows in Los Angeles. At 2 hours and 45 minutes long, the film was similar to a typical night on the tour.

The film premiered in Los Angeles on October 11. It had the highest-grossing opening weekend of any concert film in US history. An extended version was later released on streaming giant Disney+.

Swift's career continued to skyrocket. Her successful Eras Tour led her to become a billionaire in October 2023. *Speak Now (Taylor's Version)* and *1989 (Taylor's Version)* soared to the top of the charts in 2023. In December, *Time* named her its Person of the Year.

With this honor, Swift joined the ranks of public figures from presidents to popes. By the year's end, her Eras Tour became the top-grossing concert tour ever. It had earned more than $1 billion.

Swift kept the Eras Tour party going around the world in 2024. On February 16, she performed for 96,000 fans in Melbourne, Australia. It was the biggest crowd of her career. She broke more records with the April 19 release of her eleventh studio album, *The Tortured Poets Department*. It was the first in history to have more than 300 million streams on Spotify in one day. The deluxe version had 31 tracks, which was more than any of Swift's previous albums.

## WHO ARE SWIFTIES?

**According to polls, 53 percent of American adults identify as Taylor Swift fans. Millennials make up the biggest age group. Slightly more than half are female. Slightly less than 75 percent are white, with 13 percent Black and 9 percent Asian.**

# TAYLOR'S LIFE IN NUMBERS

Taylor Swift has broken records and won many awards during her career. What do you notice about these numbers? What do they tell you about Swift's life and career?

**14** No. 1 albums, more than any female artist

**81** weeks at No. 1 on *Billboard* 200 chart

**4** Album of the Year Grammy Awards

**14** total Grammy Awards

First concert tour to make **$1 BILLION**

**14** top spots at one time on the *Billboard* Hot 100

**12** No. 1 songs on the *Billboard* Hot 100

Favorite number is **13**

**11** studio albums

**4** live albums

**4** Taylor's Version re-releases

**13** documentaries and concert movies

**5** feature film acting roles

Numbers current as of July 2024

## TAYLOR SWIFT'S LEGACY

Taylor Swift has come a long way since her childhood on a Christmas tree farm. But her passion for music, strong work ethic, and belief in herself have remained unchanged. Despite becoming a global superstar, Swift has stayed true to her goal of constantly creating and innovating within the music industry. She has worked to make the world a better, more supportive place. Some have described her as providing light in a world with many divisions.

## EXPLORE ONLINE

Chapter Five explores the huge success of Taylor Swift's Eras Tour. The website below shares some of the tour's effects. Is the information from the website the same as the information in Chapter Five? What new information did you learn from the site?

### THE ERAS TOUR

abdocorelibrary.com/taylor-swift

# IMPORTANT DATES

**December 13, 1989**
Taylor Alison Swift is born in Reading, Pennsylvania.

**2006**
Swift releases her first album, *Taylor Swift*.

**2010**
Swift wins her first Grammy Awards. She wins four awards, including both Album of the Year and Best Country Album for *Fearless*.

**October 2014**
Swift releases her first fully pop album, *1989*. It debuts at No. 1 on the *Billboard* 200 chart.

**June 2015**
Swift protests Apple Music's plan to not pay artists for their songs during new subscribers' three-month free trial period. She wins the battle, ensuring all musicians are paid during that time for their work.

**2020**
The COVID-19 pandemic hits. Swift releases two albums, *Folklore* in July and *Evermore* in December.

**2023**
Swift launches her Eras Tour on March 17 in Glendale, Arizona. Her concert film *Taylor Swift: The Eras Tour* premieres in October. She is named *Time* magazine's Person of the Year in December.

**February 4, 2024**
Swift becomes the first musician ever to win four Album of the Year Grammy Awards with her win for *Midnights*.

# STOP AND THINK

## Another View

This book explores Swift's path to becoming a musician and an entertainer. As you know, every source is different. Ask a librarian or another adult to help you find a second source about Swift's life. Write a short essay comparing and contrasting the new source's point of view with that of this book's author. What is the point of view of each author? How are they similar and why? How are they different and why?

## Why Do I Care?

Taylor Swift has been a star since she was a teenager. Most teenagers won't experience fame. But there may be aspects of her life that people can relate to. What elements of her life or her beliefs do you feel a connection to? How might her creative works have an impact on people's lives around the world?

## Tell the Tale

Chapter Three of this book describes Swift's experience with streaming services, including Spotify and Apple Music.

Imagine that you have just received the news that you won't be paid for your work for three months. Write 200 words about what you could do to change this policy. How could you get this message out to the world?

## Take a Stand

As a public figure, Swift feels it is her responsibility to speak out about causes that are important to her. Some causes she is passionate about include fair practices in the music industry, LGBTQ rights, and putting an end to sexual harassment. Many people use social media outlets to promote causes that matter to them. Do you think this is a good way to make change in the world? Why or why not?

# GLOSSARY

**bill**
a proposed law presented for discussion

**bridge**
a passage that links two sections of a song

**LGBTQ**
lesbian, gay, bisexual, transgender, and queer/questioning

**marginalized**
describing people excluded from the majority group

**millennial**
a person born in the 1980s or 1990s

**nominate**
to propose for an honor, such as a musical award

**petition**
a written call for change signed by people who support the cause

**platinum**
referring to a song or an album that has sold more than one million copies

**savvy**
having practical knowledge and a good understanding of something

**shotlist**
to create a document that plans what camera shots are needed for a video

# ONLINE RESOURCES

To learn more about Taylor Swift, visit our free resource websites below.

**Core Library CONNECTION**
FREE! COMMON CORE MULTIMEDIA RESOURCES

Visit **abdocorelibrary.com** or scan this QR code for free Common Core resources for teachers and students, including vetted activities, multimedia, and booklinks, for deeper subject comprehension.

**Booklinks NONFICTION NETWORK**
FREE! ONLINE NONFICTION RESOURCES

Visit **abdobooklinks.com** or scan this QR code for free additional online weblinks for further learning. These links are routinely monitored and updated to provide the most current information available.

# LEARN MORE


Bolte, Mari. *Taylor Swift's The Eras Tour Encyclopedia*. Abdo, 2025.

Hunt, Helena, editor. *Taylor Swift in Her Own Words: Young Reader Edition*. Agate, 2024.

# INDEX



## About the Author

Alicia Z. Klepeis began her career at the National Geographic Society. A former middle school teacher, she is the author of more than 200 children's books. She loves to sing Taylor Swift songs in the car with her favorite Swiftie, her daughter.